Math Counts

Numbers

Introduction

In keeping with the major goals of the National Council of Teachers of Mathematics Curriculum and Evaluation Standards, children will become mathematical problem solvers, learn to communicate mathematically, and learn to reason mathematically by using the series Math Counts.

Pattern, Shape, and *Size* may be investigated first—in any sequence.

Sorting, Counting, and *Numbers* may be used next, followed by *Time, Length, Weight,* and *Capacity.*

Ramona G. Choos, Professor of Mathematics, Senior Adviser to the Dean of Continuing Education, Chicago State University; Sponsor for Chicago Elementary Teachers' Mathematics Club

About this Book

Mathematics is a part of a child's world. It is not only interpreting numbers or mastering tricks of addition or multiplication. Mathematics is about *ideas.* These ideas have been developed to explain particular qualities such as size, weight, and height, as well as relationships and comparisons. Yet all too often the important part that an understanding of mathematics will play in a child's development is forgotten or ignored.

Most adults can solve simple mathematical tasks without the need for counters, beads, or fingers. Young children find such abstractions almost impossible to master. They need to see, talk, touch, and experiment.

The photographs and text in these books have been chosen to encourage talk about topics that are essentially mathematical. By talking, the young reader can explore some of the central concepts that support mathematics. It is on an understanding of these concepts that a child's future mastery of mathematics will be built.

Henry Pluckrose

1995 Childrens Press® Edition
© 1994 Watts Books, London, New York, Sydney
All rights reserved.
Printed in the United States of America.
Published simultaneously in Canada.
1 2 3 4 5 6 7 8 9 0 R 04 03 02 01 00 99 98 97 96 95

Math Counts

Numbers

By Henry Pluckrose

Mathematics Consultant: Ramona G. Choos,
Professor of Mathematics

 CHILDRENS PRESS ®

CHICAGO

3

OUVERT
9ʰ A 11ʰ30 .. 14ʰ A 18ʰ.
LE SAMEDI DE 9ʰ A 11ʰ

There are numbers
all around us.
There are numbers
on houses

4

NEW HAMPSHIRE

MONTH NO. 9

NEW HAMPSHIRE 88 591667

838849

Live Free or Die

and on cars.

You can find numbers
on telephones

DIALATRON

1
2
3
4
5
6
7
8
9
* MUTE
0
REDIAL

RESET

and on money.

WEST   EAST

INTERSTATE   INTERSTAT
KANSAS   KANSAS
70   70

Numbers help us in many ways.
How does this road sign
help drivers?

These buses have route numbers.
How does this help passengers?

Numbers give information.
The numbers on these cartons
tell us how much milk
each one holds.

10

These shoes have a number
printed inside.
What do the numbers tell you?
What is your shoe size?

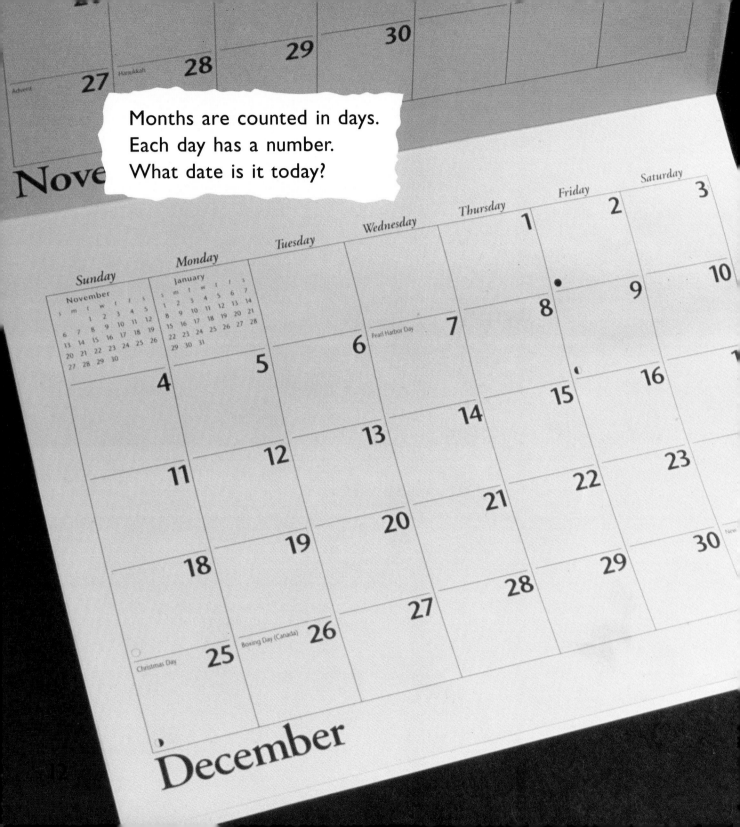

Months are counted in days.
Each day has a number.
What date is it today?

Do you know the date
of your birthday?
How old are you?

Numbers make it easier
for us to measure things.
We can use numbers
to give information.
What time is it?

How fast is the car traveling?

C F

50 120
40 100
30 80
20 60
10 40
0   20
10 0
20 20

dinlex

What is the temperature?

5 feet

How tall is this girl?

2 feet

14'-0"

We use numbers
when we measure height

and when we measure length.

636 kg
SALTER

We use numbers
when we measure weight

$ 006.45

and when we measure liquids.

GALLONS

PRICE

006.326

$

21

We use numbers in sport so that each person is easy to identify.

Which car is leading in this race?

Each player has
a different number on his shirt.
The spectators buy programs
when they go to the game.
The program tells them the names
and numbers of the players.

The scoreboard uses numbers to show which team is winning.

Numbers also are used to show positions— first, second, and third.

2

1

3

21·03

The scoreboard gives the order
in which the runners finished the race.
What do the other numbers show?

400 METRES.

1 S HEARD
2 M SOLOMON
3 P BROWN
4 D JENKINS
5 M PAUL
6 B CARERON
7 S SCUTT
  C HAMILTON

**6% GRADE
7 MILES**

**SPEED
LIMIT
25
mph
40
km/h**

**Indianapolis
161 KILOMETERS
100 MILES**

14'-11"

**LOW
CLEARANCE**

↕14FT.11IN↕

What do the numbers
in these pictures tell us?

St Michael ®

MADE IN MAURITIUS

AGE	TO FIT CHEST
5-6	23in

TOUR DE POITRINE

58cm

↓ 12 FT. 2 in

4
3
2
1
G
LG
SR

1.2m

Stovepipe Wells	22 mi	35 km
Jct (136)	83 mi	134 km
Jct 395	97 mi	156 km

How many numbers
can you see here?
What do they mean?

74

Can you imagine
what the world would be like
without numbers?

Peter Wood
74 North Street
Redding
Isle of Wight
UK
PO33 1HX

1995 Childrens Press® Edition
© 1994 Watts Books, London, New York, Sydney
All rights reserved.
Printed in the United States of America.
Published simultaneously in Canada.
1 2 3 4 5 6 7 8 9 0 R 04 03 02 01 00 99 98 97 96 95

Library of Congress Cataloging-in-Publication Data

Pluckrose, Henry Arthur.
    numbers / Henry Pluckrose.
      p.   cm.
    Originally published: London; New York: F. Watts, 1988.
    (Math counts)
    Includes index.
    ISBN 0-516-05454-6
    1. Numbers, Natural — Juvenile literature. 2. Counting — Juvenile literature. [1. Numbers,
Natural. 2. Counting.] I. Title.
QA141.3.P58   1995
513.2 — dc20   94-38007
                                                                                CIP
                                                                                AC

Photographic credits: Chris Fairclough, 4, 5, 6, 9, 11, 13, 15, 16, 18, 22, 23, 26, 29 (top left, bottom left and right), 31; Unicorn Stock Photos, © Tom McCarthy, 7, © Aneal Vohra, 8, Jim Shippee, 10, 12, © Kathryn Bellifemine, 17, © Betts Anderson, 21, 28 (top right), © Paul A. Hein, 29 (top right); ZEFA, 14, 24; Allsport © Steve Powell, 19, © London Zoo, 20; © Shaun Botterill, 25, Tony Duffy, 27; Tony Stone Images, © David R. Frazier, 28 (top left), © L.L.T. Rhodes, 28 (bottom right); PhotoEdit, © Tony Freeman, 28 (bottom left); Photri, 30

Editor: Ruth Thomson
Design: Chloë Chessman

INDEX